RETELLINGS

Stephen Brooke

Arachis Press 2013

These are stories of my life, retold.

I will not claim the poems and vignettes, the acts and scenes, presented here are in any way literal depictions of events. That makes them no less true.

©2013 Stephen Brooke

ISBN 978-1-937745-10-3

All rights reserved. The text, art and design of this publication are the copyrighted work of Stephen Brooke and may not be reproduced nor transmitted in any form without the express written permission of the author or the publisher, other than short quotes for review purposes.

Arachis Press
4803 Peanut Road
Graceville, Florida 32440
http://arachispress.com

PROLOGUE

Blender

I threw the past
in a blender—
some of this,
some of that—
and gave it a taste.

There was a memory
of strawberries
and the scents
of spice and women.
There was wine.

I had expected
bitterness,
to spit out
the flavors of pain
and regret.

There was none;
only the sad
subtle tinge
of forgotten dreams
remained, mixed

with some of this
and some of that.

ACT ONE

The Tree

The house was empty, except for the Christmas tree.

Though I was still four months shy of my third birthday, I remember it clearly. It is the first Christmas I can recall, the Christmas we spent in the tourist cottages beneath the Australian pines, our little house not quite ready yet.

But Dad set up a tree in the bare living room, placed our presents beneath it, and we all went over on Christmas morning to open them. I remember a toy truck. Or was it a fire engine? I pushed it all over the empty rooms, across the terrazzo floors. I also remember being loath to pick it up because I wasn't sure it was for me.

I was new to Christmas, after all. It's the first gift I remember receiving at any time. My parents assured me it was mine and an older sibling was not going to take it from me.

We had left Ohio a couple months earlier, just as winter was moving in. I do have a few memories of our home in the north and, in particular, everyone getting into the car on a cold day to start a trip. Was there snow or is that a detail my imagination added? I assume it was the family setting out for Florida.

Florida—that's where the memories truly begin, with a Christmas tree and an empty house.

Leap of Faith

It was miles down.

Or so it seemed to a three-year-old. Years later, I saw that cliff was no more than four or five foot, my father's arms could have easily caught me, lifted me down. But there was no way I was going to jump.

There was no way I was going to be dashed on those rocks—okay, it was a pebbly sand bar—below. Before the mistrustful man came the mistrustful kid. Then, as now, I had trouble 'reading' people. Even my dad.

We had returned to Ohio for a few weeks, a vacation of sorts and a tying up of loose ends. Our temporary home, that summer, was the 'Hill Farm,' my late grandfather's place in the Hocking Hills. I remember little else of our time there.

But that little event down at the bend of our creek, where a deeper swimming hole had been carved from the rock and sand, the work of uncounted spring floods, carved itself into me. I even had nightmares later of peering out over that cliff, while voices cajoled me to take the leap. No, Mom. No, Dad. I'm not ready to die!

Ha, I always knew you liked my little brother better.

And that is the other memory of that summer, of that stay in the hills. My brother. Sickly, whiny little brat, being fussed over by sisters and mom. I do recall going off into another room and crying because they didn't seem to love me anymore. And here I'd always been my big sisters' favorite plaything, their real, live doll.

Feeling sorry for myself—the first time I can recall but certainly not the last.

No

My first word, I am told, was 'no,'
and apparently it served

me well enough I didn't bother
with many others until I was

around four. It's still my favorite.

'Possum

The purple rabbit had lost
its floppy ears so I told
everyone it was a 'possum.

I knew all about 'possums
because my mom read me
those Mother West Wind booksand I saw the pictures
of ol' Unc' Billy Possum
and there wasn't much else

my earless purple bunny
resembled. At least nothing
else in a five-year-old's experience.

I did know a purple 'possum
makes a good friend. Better
than my brother's pink bear,

anyway. Way better.

Mosquitoes

The screen was thick with mosquitoes.

We did not close our jalousie windows to the night. This was before air conditioning was common in Florida, when electric fans moved the heavy Gulf air from one room to another.

Too many mosquitoes, too many sand flies, to sleep outside, though the spray truck drove through the neighborhood each evening, leaving a white fog of insecticide lingering along the street. It knocked down some of the insects, I'm sure, but who knows what that mist did to our own lungs?

Especially those youngsters who would ride their bicycles behind the truck, dodging in and out of the fog.

Dad knew where to escape the bugs and maybe escape a houseful of rug-rats, as well. He was down at the pier, fishing, and we kids wouldn't see him till tomorrow morning. There might be a couple more snook fillets in the refrigerator, waiting to be deep-fried for our supper.

We actually grew tired of snook, as delicious as it can be. Dad gave away more than he brought home.

I might have been three, I might have been four. The story is the same, the little house on the curve of the road, empty, white sand lots on all sides, where nothing grew but sand spurs. We sat by the jalousie window at night, framed by the maroon drapes with their abstract patterns, Fifties-style, rounded rectangles like little TV screens.

And in the dark beyond them, as Mom read a bedtime story, the mosquitoes buzzed.

Moving On

Death was in the fields
that January,
as the cattle lay down
all along the highway
out of town.
Feverish with mumps,
I too lay down,
listened to the winter rain
beat at the roof of our
oh-so-ugly red and white
Plymouth station wagon.
We were moving on
once again.

Maple

Clinging to those highest branches
I could see no more, truly,
than from my window.

But to eight-year-old eyes,
the world looks different
from the top of a maple.

It's branches took me
in a wooden embrace,
less comfortable

than chairs, but greener.
Whirly-gig seed pods
found the welcoming soil;

I never fell, except
into the sky.

Holes In the Linoleum

I could have counted the holes but never bothered. There were more close to my bed than elsewhere in the room, rough lines of punctures in the gray and blue linoleum.

Beneath each line lay a gap in the century-old weathered floorboards, a crevice that spoke of settling foundations, out-of-plumb carpentry. At eight years of age, I didn't really think much of such things. I just knew the house was old, that my father had slept there as a boy. That was far enough back to be somewhere in a dim antiquity.

The bed I shared with my little brother was tippy—a cot with sides that folded out. Looking back, I can see that we could have simply slid a box or such under the sides to keep it from tipping over when one or the other got up or moved too close to the edge. Why no one ever did that, I don't know.

Were they all simply too busy, too wrapped up in themselves, to bother, to even notice? I know it was a time when my parents were scraping out a living, commuting sixty miles to Columbus each day, while we lived on my late grandfather's farm. I didn't remember my grandfather.

I do remember my mom, arriving home after dark, coming up to the bedroom to say goodnight. My sisters would already have made us supper. I and my older brother and sometimes the little one, too, would go down to the cellar and bring up potatoes. Some would almost always be rotting and we would throw them, stinking missiles, into the night before returning to the warm kitchen and its coal-burning stove.

And Mom, still in the high heels she wore to work, would come to our room. The room was up the steep narrow staircase, on the back of the house where I would see the sun burnishing the sandstone cliffs when I awoke. Those heels, narrow and spiky—she never seemed to remember what they could do to the linoleum. Maybe she was too tired to think of it.

A heel would land on a crack and open up another hole and Mom would remember then. Too late, and she might show her annoyance with herself and that floor and that house for a moment, before saying 'good night' and turning off the light.

Cliffs

'A bear's been here,' he said, pointing to the torn pine, but even at eight I knew enough to suspect my brother of having snuck up here, sometime before I woke, and using his hatchet. Still, I kept a watchful eye as we climbed slowly, the path growing steeper among the trees, up to the cliffs, the sandstone terraces, the vultures' apartment house.

I would watch them from my wood-framed window, the little bedroom at the back of the farmhouse, leaning out to see them rise, soar from the rock ledges, into the summer sky. You couldn't really see their nests from the top of the cliffs, though, even if one were foolish enough—or had a negligent brother—to edge out to the edge and look over.

No doubt it wasn't as far down as I remember but it would have broken my eight-year old neck, all the same. The vultures would surely have approved.

Chicks

In Spring, the mailman brings chickens.
They were ordered weeks ago, following
much study of the Sears catalog.
This one's a good layer, said Dad.
Lets get at least fifty. Mom nodded;
she would be the one to fill out
the order blank, torn from the middle
of the thick catalog, write out a check
that wouldn't break a farmer's budget.
Dad and Mike have repaired the coop
(which shares a roof with the outhouse)
and now we wait. And wait! I cleaned
up the feeder and water tank myself;
Mom says we will place marbles in the water
so the chicks drink. They're pretty stupid
and need something shiny to catch
their attention. A bit like my brother.

Stephen Brooke

They'll come while I'm at school,
probably, after the bus carries me
around the long gravel loop, past farm houses,
past the budding apple orchards and over
that final hill. A couple of cardboard boxes
with holes in the top so they can breathe,
soft peeping from the darkened interior.
The carrier here knows all about baby chicks
in the mail. He's been at it for a lot of Springs.
I've been helping plan the garden and Dad
says I can be responsible for feeding
the chicks when they come. We ordered
weeks ago and now the weather
is getting warmer so it's safe for them
to travel by mail. They'll come soon—
in Spring the mailman brings chickens.

Martha

'Martha's dead.'

I didn't understand.
Weren't we playing
yesterday, on the back steps?

'Martha's dead,'
solemn eight-year-olds
whispered to each other.

'Diabetes,' not sure what
that was, nor death,
for that matter.

On the swings,
I sailed as high as I could
to hide my tears.

Along the Road

Every year, another town,
another house—not a home,

just a stop along our road.
A new school, new bunch of guys

to beat on me. As if I didn't
get enough of that already.

Did it make me what I am
or did I make it what it was?

Every forest has its paths,
though we may blaze them for ourselves.

Did the lad who was lost,
who learned to walk behind his wit

and his fists, always live there,
along the road to somewhere else?

Test Tubes

I had test tubes. Chemistry,
science. That was the thing
when I was a kid. I could

have been a chef, you know.
But no, the adults said,
that's not for you. You can

do better. It wasn't what
we were, then, before Emeril
or Wolfgang. Even before

Graham galloped across
television screens.
Oh, we had Julia, of course,

and her impeccably clean
purple towel. Although
the TV was black and white.

You can do better. College.
Maybe for the rest
of my life. Get a post.

No need to ever leave.
And so, I had test tubes.
But I never cooked up

anything I really
wanted in them.

Shorthand

She learned shorthand as a girl,
whether Gregg or Pitman
I couldn't tell you.

Does anyone bother these days
to master those squiggles,
a secret secretary language?

Her notes and grocery lists
were indecipherable,
mysteries to a child.

They could mean anything
with enough imagination—
Christmas gifts

or coded messages
to the spy ring that had
planted her here.

A mole, pretending
to be my mom—
nah, maybe not,

for it wasn't difficult
to read the shorthand
of a mother's love.

ACT TWO

Wild Guavas

Along the abandoned railroad tracks where the palmetto had been cleared away and not yet reclaimed its domain, its scrub country birthright, we came to gather wild guavas. My brother and I brought buckets and bags and a twenty-two to plink at the empty cans we found. We always found cans, mostly beer but sometimes soda. Either works for target practice.

But the guavas, that's why we came: sweet and tart, full of worms but free and the worms didn't matter once they were cooked down with plenty of sugar. I know about the guava jelly and the paste found at stores or those roadside stands for the tourists but there's nothing better than homemade guava preserves topping a bowl of vanilla ice cream. That's how Florida tasted to me.

We gathered as many as we could find, as many as we could carry home; there Mom took charge and filled the house with their aroma, simmering in the big dented stock pot and even outdoors we'd catch that perfume sifting through the open jalousie windows.

It's been too many years since I picked a wild guava, a long time since I was a boy with a bag and a rifle and an eye out for snakes and I don't know if they grow there anymore.

But they did; they did, back then.

Priests

Father Joe lit up another stogy. He wasn't your typical priest; no, he'd been married and a shopkeeper up north, somewhere. But his wife had died and he had turned, searching, to the church.

I liked his cigar.

The stink of it reminded me of sitting with my grandfather. It made him someone I could talk to, not like the career clergy, the ones who'd been priests inside since the sixth grade.

I should be a priest, I was told, a priest.

Even my unbeliever father thought so. You're too unworldly. The Church will take care of you.

I knew better. I knew long before the other boys my age. Old Father Joe listened and may even have understood, beneath an ancient banyan in the church yard.

He'd never become a member of the priests' club—always an assistant at some small parish or another, where the children loved him and the adults wondered just what the bishop had foisted on them this time.

He rose from the bench beside me to hop-scotch on the sidewalk with girls who could have been his granddaughters if God hadn't played the old switch game with him.

Sometimes, I feel like lighting up a cigar just in memory of Father Joe, let some of that familiar incense rise.

You know, I gave them up a while back.

Banyan

I.

Me and a guy and another guy
were hanging down at the pier
or in the parking lot, to be exact,
where that big banyan latticed
its trailing roots across the shade.

By mid-morning the heat and the sun
and the wind turning onshore
would send us to its shelter,
and later the rain would come
and it served as our leaky umbrella,

while we watched the tourists
run to their cars and the girls,
the older girls who paid no attention
to three sunburned surf-rats,
turned their faces to the shower.

We gave them the eye, though,
those girls in their summer tans,
or the corner of the eye,
and maybe they appreciated
the admiration or maybe not.

The older guys would have said
things, did say things when they
hung there in the evening,
but we only thought them
and felt cooler for doing so.

II.

The sidewalk had been shoved up,
broken into concrete triangles
and trapezoids and other shapes
that could be described mathematically
by someone else, gray where they

had not been stained by the rain
percolating through the leaves
and sand had crept across,
to be removed now-and-again
by someone from the city crew.

Ten-thousand thong-sandals
would know that abstract-expressionist
collage, a season's work for tree
and wind and rain to create
from bits and pieces left by man

and a season's work to make anew.
I had counted the seasons beneath
the banyan, knowing they would add
up to something, someday, a sum
of summers, all in a column.

A column of rising cloud, over
the Gulf, promised thunderstorms.
That, too, was summer and the sum
of all a day was to me, then,
when the lightning painted the sky.

III.

In the night, I have seen the banyan
and none beneath it but the lone
drinker, taking solace in darkness
and muscatel. In the night,
as I detoured on the way home

from my job, I would remember
my addition and wonder whether
I totaled it up all wrong.
The answer was always too high
for it to matter, anyway.

They tore down the old hotel
to expand the parking lot
and put in meters and a guard
and no one hangs out there now
or sits in screened porches

watching what used to be
over gin and tonic and citronella.
The girls are still there, though,
and their bikinis smaller than when
I was a kid skating

the bumpy sidewalk to the banyan.
That's illegal now, too,
but the surf still blows out by late
morning and it still rains
almost every summer afternoon.

Trip

As ribbons of light chase ribbons of wave to the horizon, we whisper. Outa control. Maybe up at Canaveral it's surfable.

A Sixty-two Corvair on A-1-A, a winter morning, a winter swell; a monster swell and we are not the kids to attempt the ride. No, not at Monster Hole. We can see surfers there, a few specks in the valley of the swell, from atop Sebastian bridge. We know that even the paddle out would be too much for us.

Head north. North past the joggers waking themselves in the wind. North past Patrick, where no one is practicing landings this morning.

At least it's still offshore, my brother mutters and we nod but maybe we'd just as soon the wind came around and broke the back of this swell, made it unrideable, and we could sit in the Krystal eating breakfast chili and taking comfort in coffee.

Canaveral. Jetty Park. Last chance—we can't drive any further along the coast and, hey, it's not bad! My new Rick should handle these just fine and Pat has his magic board and so what if half the kids in Cocoa are out in it?

So what if my morning classes are a hundred miles in my past?

It's Nineteen and Sixty-nine and any trip is good.

Any trip at all.

Dorm Room 1970

We laughed between our kisses
and swigs of Boone's Farm,
as Taj Mahal sang
the Volkswagen Blues.
You were another guy's,
not mine;

no, never mine.

Two kids in an empty
weekend dorm,
We shared your boyfriend's
stash and pretended
we weren't lonely
all night.

Fruta

Little Maria has picked all the raisins
out of her oatmeal and laid each one, each
small unknown object, beside the pink bowl.

It is her favorite bowl. She has never
seen raisins before this morning and thinks
they might be bugs. She does not eat bugs,

being a sensible and smart *muchacha*,
as four-year-olds go. With my limited Spanish,
I can not convince her that they are just *fruta*,

that they are *buena*. Maria can be
stubborn and little dark wrinkled *frutas*
have not been a part of her life nor her breakfast.

Ah well, the twins, Raul and Diego, have filled
their chubby cheeks with her rejects. They like
raisins. I think they may even like bugs.

Pier

Two middle-aged women down by the pier
were the only ones on the beach and I
watched them a while from the van, as they
fed the wind-riding gulls, and I watched

the waves too, before getting my board
and my wet-suit out, wondering
if the wind was too much but it was from
the side and the form wasn't that bad.

There would be others along. They'd check
me out and if I caught a few
they'd hit it too. Not many kids.
It was a school day and they would save

their hookies for sunnier mornings, better
waves, just as they would one day
have steady jobs and let the boards
rot in the garage while they vacationed

at Disney with their own kids and I
would still be in the water of gray
windy mornings, letting the world
get on with all it thought important.

The Beach ~ Summer

Those were summer nights on the beach—
the stars would crowd our sky, phosphorescent waves
tumbled, faded about the piles of the pier.

I remember the pier, its floating lights,
and I remember distant lightning over the Gulf
and the lightning of Fourth of July fireworks.

Has it grown too late to spread a blanket
on the sugar sand, to play my guitar
once more, softly, for the night?

For the night and for you—ah, youth
was never that sweet yet I remember
the way a summer night should be.

The Beach ~ Winter

Gray solitude—the wind sprayed
its name across the walls of winter,
those crumbling ice-water arcades

where I played pinball with my soul.
It should have been a summer dalliance,
not that storm-filled affair;

the sea is a gentle lover then.
She must grow cold, grow volatile,
humbling we who paid her court

and paid her toll. Each summer lover
fell away till I remained—
I in her gray solitude.

Come, Sit With Me

The sky hangs heavy, cloudless,
the deep, dry blue of Spring
fading to the sea.
Today, I have accomplished
little, but enjoyed much.
Come, sit with me, my friend;
the breeze is cool and salty;
we'll share my wine as day
softens into evening.

Scars

This scar is from the time
my dirt bike fell on me
on a sand road back behind
the new high school. Yeah, Lely—
I did sub teaching there

later, when I was older
but not much wiser.
That bike threw me more
than once; I'm just too clumsy,
I guess, to go that fast.

Give me water. It's more
forgiving than sand and rocks,
though I've been bounced off the bottom
a few times too, felt the sting
of salt water wounds.

The only visible reminder
would be this lop-sided toe
I broke. Nothing like the scar
on my leg, the one from the bike,
nor my much-broken nose.

That's another story
but I'm always happy
to talk about my time
in the ring and only
exaggerate a little.

I was no golden boy,
nor even Golden Gloves,
just a skinny kid
with long arms and no punch
who lost every fight.

Oh, and there's that seam
down the back of my skull.
If I ever develop
a bald spot it will show
but just take my word

on it for now, okay?
Not the small scar, that's where
my little brother whacked me
when I was six and he
was a terrible brat.

I reckon he never grew
out of that, but I
digress. The long scar there,
that's the one I got
when a cable broke

in the gym and the pulldown
bar slammed into the back
of my noggin. I should
have sued, I suppose, but, hey,
the owner was a friend.

Oh, that one? I didn't
know it showed. Every
wound that heals must leave
a scar, a little mark,
a bit of stiffness to remind

us to be more careful.
Maybe next time, I
should not go quite so fast,
ride the smaller wave,
stay out of the ring,

Stephen Brooke

not risk a broken heart.
But then, what would the point
of living be? I shall show
my every scar, wear them
on my skin, my face,

my soul, let them be
the handwriting of time,
the tale of who I am
and who I will be,
come my next scar.

Key Limes

The last key limes have browned,
refrigerated, saved
for one more sip of Summer,
a season already passed.

Too long I waited, too long,
while Autumn's broom swept color
here and there and then
away to leave only gray.

The bottled stuff must do,
I guess, or bagged-up lemons
from the super-market;
those I can find all Winter.

I'll not complain for there
will be another year,
another crop of limes,
another taste of sun.

Red Tide

Where the fish form
a stinking silver mat
that bumps against
the shoreline, crabs feast,

not knowing—for crabs
are not knowing creatures—
that they too die, poisoned
by the rust-red sea.

I've seen it before;
I know the Gulf, grew up
on these sands. I know
I will see it again.

Nature's cycle: the red tide
must come on a summer wind,
when phosphorescent waves
tumble into the night,

when monsoon and heat
set a kettle boiling
out there. It's been happening
since there were seas.

I've seen it before;
but have we now,
with our cities, our waste,
tipped this balance too far?

My eyes are full
of the acrid breeze,
the wheeling glutton gulls.
On the deserted beach

and out along the limestone
groin, more dead fish
rise and fall with the whispering
swells of summer.

One Moment

In one decisive moment, she jumped from the rust-bucket car as it paused at the corner. In one decisive moment, I became protector, knight-in-shining-armor, for a drunken redneck chick who bore the wounds of her drunken redneck man and had used that decisive moment to do something about it.

I kept a .38 tucked in the back of my trousers, under my jacket, a snub-nose Harrington and Richardson I had prayed I would never need to pull. The cops knew I carried it and winked at the illegality—they knew the streets, too.

And I stood there, her behind me, looking at this car where half-a-dozen or maybe eight drunken rednecks were looking back at me and I looked at my one stoned buddy who didn't seem to quite grasp the situation and thought again of that H and R and did not like the thought.

But only her abuser stepped out to confront me, a little Charlie Manson sort of guy and drunk as shit and I knew I could take him out with two or three punches if he didn't have a gun himself, or knife, and he stood there, staring me down, I guess, until he said, *The hell with it* and got back in and they lurched away.

A deputy showed up soon after I called and drove my damsel in distress off and I don't know why but I asked about her later and was told the husband picked her up and she never charged him.

It was no longer my concern, anyway, and I can't remember what she looked like but I remember him and I remember the fear that I might do something that would ride with me into eternity.

Stephen Brooke

ACT THREE

Downtown Bar, 2 PM Slot

Waves of heat line dance
above the crowded pavements
of a Nashville afternoon.
Behind cool worlds of glass,

where neon curves dimly
into mirrored names,
I watch phantoms shimmer
among the tourists

and play your blues for tips
and a cold one.
At the far, dark end
of the bar, Jimmy waits

his turn. He's in no hurry.
His father was a Name
in this town;
Jim just plays guitar

and drinks too much.
Me, I am drunk on delusion—
It's easy to come by
in Music City.

At the fulcrum of my life,
I sit in a downtown bar,
another forty-year-old
who misplaced tomorrow.

I won't find it along my streets
of summer; I won't find it here.
Your Cheating Heart becomes
a memory, hung on these walls.

Pickles

Two AM,
five pickles
in a Krystal carton.
That's four burgers—
one had doubles.

Not that it matters,
I don't eat them anyway.
No more chili, but maybe
a refill on coffee.
De-caf, this time;

It is Two AM,
after all
(I said that, didn't I?),
and I've already had enough
to make my hands shake

and I've read all the paper
and there won't be another
for two hours
or so.
I could drive out I-40

toward Lebanon
(they really do have cedars there)
and catch a few hours sleep
in the rest area.
Try to catch a few hours

with parking lot lights
shining in my van windows
and my mind full
of the night
and tomorrow.

Another Sunny Day

The captains always come in early
for coffee at a corner table;
they must complain about the wind
and wonder where the fish have gone.

But dawn will draw them to the docks,
if they have charters booked today,
or want to get out of the house
and think the catch could pay their gas.

The fog lifts from this morning slowly—
we'll have another sunny day,
with nothing special going on;
there's no place else I need to be.

And some, I know, would say my life
is little more than wasted time;
I've crossed a sea of faded dreams
to lose myself upon this shore.

Now, most days, I will sit and doze
till all my dreams have run together;
they melt and mix and flow away
like watercolors in the rain.

Gulf Coast

Morning has come to this old Gulf coast town,
Little to do, no where else I am bound;
Sunrise to sunset, my life will go on,
Fishing and sitting right here in the sun.
I guess that I might as well stay around,
It's as good as any place I have found.

Cedars

'Why y'plantin' weeds?' asks my brother.

I ignore him. Or, rather, I give him that weary don't-bug-me-I'm-busy look he should know by now, and go back to transplanting cedar saplings.

Sure, around here, as in most of the South, the red cedar is a weed. It sprouts in pastures, it spreads into pine plantations. The tree just plain is a survivor; that's why I'm putting in a hedge of them. Nothing grows as readily in our sparse sandy soil.

Except maybe sandspurs and saw palmettos—those I could do without.

They make a quite handsome tree as they grow. At first they have the Christmas tree look about them. Alas, they do not do well in that role, once cut; the needles fall far too quickly. When more mature, they spread their gnarled limbs, harboring the tiny darting Blue-gray Gnatcatchers.

And, in the season, the Cedar Waxwings come to gorge on their berries. Ah, those pungent blue berries! The tree is actually a juniper, you know. Yes, they're the flavoring in gin.

So, on a cool autumn day, with rain in the air, I find myself planting young cedars beside the drive. Some will not make it, I know; some will grow into beauties in a surprisingly short time.

When I am done, tools put away, the soil washed from me by a welcome hot shower, I will toast the 'weeds.' With gin, of course.

My Sister's Kitchen

I drink my sister's weak coffee,
wondering, into the dawn,
of God's chemistries that make
us almost one and his spirits
that have us so unalike.

On my way to somewhere,
my van sits in her drive, one night.
On my way to somewhere
she doesn't live, I'll find
a road across the sunrise.

And, in time, I'll find myself
here once more in this kitchen
or perhaps never again drink
my sister's coffee. She can't
make coffee worth a damn.

Post Office

I'd go anyway, for my mail.
It's only a mile, minutes
by bike when the weather's good.
But I choose my time,

to be there when she is.
We check our boxes, side
by side, exchange a greeting.
Then she drives away,

wheels her Mustang (who paid
for it?) out of the lot,
back to the house on the river
that I will never ride by.

I stand there a moment,
going through my letters
(any checks today?)
before I pedal home.

Bamboo

Bamboo, like fences, makes good neighbors—
or maybe it just makes good fences.
Good honey, too, if you've a mind
to keep bees. I go to a stand
up the road for mine, of course.

Twelve canes I planted last Fall, along
the line,to hide what they would.
At least one has rooted. Someday,
I may regret the bamboo thicket
that will surely grow, persistent,
impenetrable, gold-green shafts
that hold the shadow and the sun, that whisper
wordless haiku to the wind.

For now, I just want it to screen
my neighbor, to make him a good
neighbor, yes, the kind with a fence,
to give me privacy when I
roam the house unencumbered
of clothes, come sweltering summer nights.

Come on, don't you do that?
Oh well, you do have family there
and your bamboo is neatly potted.
I would live in a grove, a forest,
if I could, shutting out
the world's eyes. I would dwell
there the way you dwell in my heart.

Berries

Today's work can be
tomorrow's work
but blackberries ripen
only once.

I know roads,
dappled dirt roads
through the pines;
bring a pail

and we will find
the sweetest berries,
the blackest berries,
in thorny shadow.

One for the bucket,
one for the mouth;
the taste is worth
a scratch or two.

Come with me;
it is May
and blackberries ripen
only once.

Fireflies

The new ceiling fan
sang *Happy Birthday*,
the first night she
stayed with me.

I had moved the bed
beneath the window
and asked an April
evening in, lit

with firefly candles.
How often have I
held this memory,
flickering in

my hand, fading
like the fireflies
that danced that night
among the oaks.

Mug

I remember tasting her lips,
there in the kitchen, dogs underfoot.

She would send me into the dawn,
warmed with coffee and her kiss,

to carry me on my gray drive home.
I fill that same red travel mug

this morning, coffee and memory
still sweet and warm, and my dark drive

will take me somewhere else.

Arts and Crafts

We'd always made our pilgrimages
to the outdoor art shows
so I wasn't surprised to see you there,
new boyfriend in tow, bored but willing.

Oh, I knew about him, one friend
or another has kept me in the loop,
even if you haven't. Last year,
it was my hand you held,

as you paused at each jeweler's display,
apologizing for taking so much time
and smiling that smile that use to tear
my heart in little pieces and paste it back together,

when I said 'No problem, kid.
When are you going to start making
your own again?' 'Soon, I have
too much to do at work right now.'

Polite hellos, shaking hands,
as Hank Williams songs went through my mind.
'I can't help it if I'm still in love with you.'
Am I? Yeah, sure, but the fire only smolders.

Even then, I guess I realized
we were all wrong. I didn't care.
I was in love; that was all that mattered.
'Good to see you.' 'How have you been?'

Stephen Brooke

'This is Barry.' 'Pleased to meet you.'
The hell I am. Oh well, I came
knowing I might bump into you.
Knowing there is no paste now for my heart.

Hardee's

I drove past
a Hardee's today.
No big deal, huh?

Except it was
the place we met, wearing
our very best smiles,

and it still
hurts as I go past
my past.

Tuskegee Haibun

The students at Tuskegee chatter as they walk past Booker T. Washington's resting place. The marker has become a part of their everyday life, seen but not seen. In the late afternoon, the cross atop the chapel casts its shadow across the small plot of graves.

passers-by
no longer notice
the old grave

The chapel is tall and angular, pointing to the Alabama sky. Inside, a pianist practices for her evening performance. This is why I have come so far.

three hundred miles
to hear a piano
played well

I set up a pair of microphones to record. It is no great skill, yet suddenly people become deferential. I am, of a sudden, doctor, shaman, possessor of arcane knowledge.

the engineer
fusses with his settings
for effect

Bach and Liszt, waltzes and hymns: the music rises into the scalloped vault. I check my levels from time to time, then listen. This is music I do not wish to experience through headphones. After the applause—lower the volume—I pack for the long drive back. Soon, I am on the road, stopping only at the rest areas for coffee and snacks.

vending machine
sells Moon Pies ~
almost home

Crossing the St John's

Dawn was but a whisper of rose
when I crossed the river, the wide
St John's that slowly, darkly flows.
A city slept on either side,

slept and dreamed while I traversed
the empty hours of the night.
In silence still it lay immersed
as I journeyed toward the light,

faint and far, beyond this span;
at ocean's edge I'd find the sun.
Beneath me, now, the St John's ran,
hours marked since I'd begun,

pilgrim to a distant shore.
A whisper of rose before me lay
and I'd less than an hour more
to the Atlantic and the day.

The Piano Player

I'm with the piano player.
You've seen me now
and then at gigs, haven't you?
I fetch her a plate from the buffet,
stand in the background,

and I've had these *hesitation blues*
far too long. Oh, yes, I've had them
but I'm with the piano player
despite the water that's run
under every bridge between us.

That's a lot of bridges and a lot
of water and too much time,
some would say, to hesitate.
Let God have His mysterious ways;
I'm with the piano player.

ACT FOUR

Crooked House

The humped beams beneath the floor
throw the kitchen off balance. I walk
drunkenly. There is dirt
on the shelves and drawers full of cold.

Time clings to the walls; it is
all echoes and dim mirrors here.
Nothing is new. The windows whisper
into the caverns of the night.

I would settle like these foundations,
change as slowly as the fields,
filled with seasons of growth and sleep.
I'd bank the embers of my dreams.

The roof is bowed by long conversations
with the insistent rain. Will I
stay, they wonder now, a crooked
man, come home to a crooked house?

There is a porch, with room to drowse,
room to remember and to forget,
and each post is a bit askew.
Tomorrow can come by and sit.

We've things to talk about, and sky
to look at. I have watched the crows fly
and they take a crooked path
from here to somewhere over there.

Dolphins

There were dolphins
and glow-in-the-dark
stars on the walls.
That and pink paint—
the room was bare,
empty of furniture,
empty of the girl
who had lived there,
who had watched the stars
slowly dim
as she fell into sleep.
Did she dream
of those dolphins,
leaping, playing
along a far-away shore?
Ah, did she dream
that she was with them,
one of them, and not
a very small girl
whose parents were losing
their home and each other?
How could I know?
All I have seen
is a pink room with dolphins
and glow-in-the-dark stars.

Ti-ti

When the ti-ti loses
its fragrance, it means
only that gardenias
will soon bloom.

Today resents not
tomorrow's arrival
nor do the seasons
regret their change.

The ti-ti may be
taller next year
but its flowers will be
just as fragrant.

My Father's Tools

All his tools are here now.

The hammers and screwdrivers,
the table saw that nearly
took my finger once.

See? Here's the scar.

There is rust: the rust
of long years' illness
and two more since his death.

They've mourned long enough.

And so, I will clean them,
shelve them, make them ready.
Who else would do it—

do this one last chore?

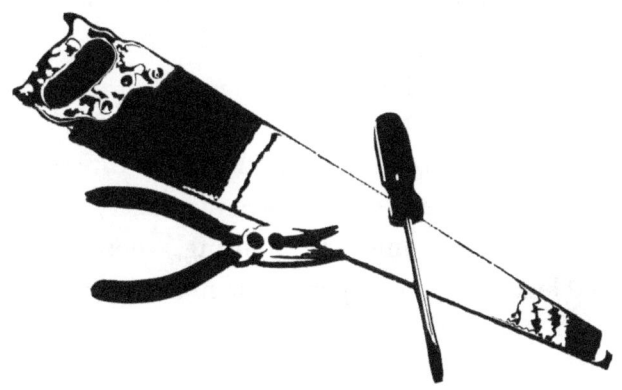

Sugar Sand

The beaches here are white, as white
as the beaches of my childhood.

I've traveled far to find these sands:
there's no return to childhood's shore.

The sweet sugar sand has washed away
into the Gulf of Memory.

The Pond

The frogs sing, come warm evenings, March or April, as rains replenish the cypress pond. It lies beyond the green curve of the neighbors' field, south-east and south-east again.

They grow cotton one year, peanuts the next, though once they threw us a curve, planting cotton two years in a row.

Ah, well, cotton is always planted in a row.

But the field—it slopes down to the pond, to the cypress, the willows and gum, and we're glad to have the music, when frogs sing, come the warm evenings. In the spring, when we can sit on the porch and leave windows open to the night, we listen.

Security Light

Due south, across the cotton field,
beyond the paper-cutout trees,
one light burns, harsh guardian
of the neighbors' barn.

Transmuted by distance, it becomes
as another star at the window,
my companion through the night.

Winter's Prison

In the fields, the ibis feed,
like snow where snow does not fall,
in the pastures where the shaggy
horses wait in timeless being.

Winter's prison has its walls,
grayer than the cold horizon,
closed as broken hearts are closed
to the hope of any Spring.

Such days are too short for hope;
I grow weary with the naming
of my losses. It is dusk
and their faces are the wind.

This, my cell, is bounded by
shadow bars the bare-branch trees
cast across the frosted windows,
fading, fading into night.

Dawn comes cold, yet there will be
sun, a memory of dream.
I, too, wait, forgetting time,
knowing only winter's prison.

Long Stories

The roof is leaking again,
I tell myself and the dog.

She'll listen to me ramble
if I say her name

now and again.
Where's my treat? she wonders

as I ramble further,
ramble from room to room, looking

for whatever I lost there.
Shouldn't I know it when I see it?

I could rearrange that shelf,
I tell myself, *or sort the laundry.*

I do talk to myself,
and the rain and the dog

tolerate the long stories
with no need to understand.

May

May arrived on a murmur of bees
and distant mowers. The wordless rains
of night had carried Spring away

and a pungency of privet
now frames the day, stinky-sweet snow
bending to a bramble embrace.

There is no purpose in such a day.
It dozes. It dreams beyond its fences
into fields of the fresh-turned future.

My Fields

The south wind brings the Gulf to my fields,
sea-scent sighing across the grass-tops.

Only the dragonfly hovers here,
motionless over waves that find

no shore, know no seabirds' cries.
Yet there is a whisper of salt in the air,

a half-remembered tale of the sun.
Fifty miles and more it is

to the Gulf, but when the wind
lies in the south, it comes to my fields.

EPILOGUE

Journeyed

I have journeyed long,
without a destination,
on restless roads of night,
in sleepless desperation.

I have yearned for peace,
somewhere, peace to last,
all the endless miles
I've raced against my past.

And I could have stopped,
pulled it over, thought
'No more, I've traveled far
enough and have found naught.

'Let life and road go on
without me at the wheel.
My eyes have longed to close;
this highway's all I feel.'

'Just a little further,
around this shadowed bend,'
whispered my heart, knowing
you were my journey's end.

On roads of night it heard;
it knew your distant song
as I traveled far,
as I journeyed long.

AUTHOR'S NOTES

The pieces in this book are roughly chronological, and grouped in 'acts' accordingly, carrying me from Ohio and southern Florida to, eventually, the Florida Panhandle where I now reside.

They were written over a fairly wide range of years; some are fresh from my pen (and I do sometimes still write on paper), others from further back. Although this leads to certain differences in style, it is my hope that my voice carries through all of them.

The illustrations here are my own work, in the sense that I created them on the computer. However, some are manipulated photographs or pictures that did not originate with me.

Stephen Brooke ©2013

www.ingramcontent.com/pod-product-compliance
Lightning Source LLC
Chambersburg PA
CBHW020021050426
42450CB00005B/589